Vegetarian Kebabs

VEGETARIAN KEBABS

Rano Suri

wisdom tree

Photographs: Ashish Chawla
Cover: Mexican Kebab

ISBN 978-81-8328-078-5

Published by
Wisdom Tree
4779/23 Ansari Road
Darya Ganj, New Delhi-110002
Ph.: 23247966/67/68
wisdomtreebooks@gmail.com

CONTENTS

KAKORI KEBAB

Ingredients
12 to 15 boiled baby potatoes
6 tsp hung curd
2 tsp lemon juice
1 tsp ginger paste
½ tsp garlic paste
¼ tsp cardamom powder
2 or 3 crushed green chillies
½ tsp *saunf* (aniseeds)
1 tsp salt
2 tsp oil
½ tsp sugar
Few mint leaves chopped finely
A pinch of cinnamon powder
A pinch of *kesar* (saffron)

• *Servings 6 persons* • *Preparation time 5 mins. + marination time*
• *Cooking time 10 mins. + 10 mins. for baking*

- Peel potatoes and thoroughly prick them all over.
- Mix all the ingredients in a bowl and rub them on the potatoes. Marinate for an hour.
- Grease a large pan and cook potatoes on high flame till dry.
- Bake them in a pre-heated oven at 200°C for 10 minutes till golden brown.
- Garnish with roasted nuts and raisins.
- Serve hot with plum chutney.

KEBAB-E-MUMTAZ

Ingredients
12 small dinner buns or rolls
6 tsp hung curd
1 tsp red chilli powder
2 tsp coriander powder
½ tsp *ajwain* (caraway seeds)
3 tsp lemon juice
2 tsp chopped onion
2 green chillies, chopped
4 tsp crushed cashewnuts
2 tsp oil
½ tsp sugar
A pinch of dry orange colour

- *Servings 6 persons*
- *Preparation time 10 mins.*
- *Baking time 12 mins.*

- Remove a thin layer from dinner rolls and keep aside.
- Mix together the rest of the ingredients, i.e. hung curd, red chilli powder, coriander powder, *ajwain*, lemon juice, orange colour, onion, green chillies, cashewnuts, oil and sugar till smooth.
- Spread a thick layer of the mixture on each bun or roll (layer-removed side).
- Bake them in a pre-heated oven at 200°C for 12 minutes.
- Serve hot. Sprinkle lemon juice. Arrange them on tomato slices. Garnish with mint leaves and lots of potato wafers.

HARA KEBAB

• *Servings 6 persons* • *Preparation time 20 mins.* • *Cooking time 20 mins.*

Ingredients

1 cup blanched spinach
½ cup boiled *channa dal*
4 tsp roasted *besan*
1 boiled and grated potato
½ cup boiled peas, roughly mashed
1 small onion, finely chopped
2 or 3 green chillies
4 tsp coriander leaves
4 bread slices chopped and churned or 1 cup fresh bread crumbs
1 tsp grated ginger
½ tsp *garam masala*
½ tsp roasted and ground *jeera* (cumin seeds)
½ tsp *amchur* (mango powder)
1 tsp salt
A clove of garlic
Oil for frying

- Squeeze the blanched spinach and chop it finely.
- Mix *channa dal*, roasted *besan*, potato, boiled peas, onion, green chillies, coriander leaves, fresh bread crumbs, ginger, garlic, ground *jeera*, *garam masala*, *amchur* and salt.
- Mix them and mash them till smooth.
- Take a small portion of the mixture. Make a round ball. Press it and shape it like a *kebab*. Similarly make all the *kebabs*.
- Fry them in hot oil till lightly golden greenish in colour.
- Serve hot with minty dip and cucumber and tomato salad.

MINTY DIP

Take ½ cup curd (beaten), 4 tsp mint chutney, a pinch of black rock salt. Mix all the ingredients.

Ingredients

100 gms soya granules (Nutrella) boiled
1 cup boiled *channa dal*
1 small finely chopped onion
2 finely chopped green chillies
4 tsp chopped coriander leaves
½ tsp red chilli powder
½ tsp roasted ground *jeera* (cumin seeds)
½ tsp *amchur* (mango powder)
½ tsp coarsely ground *saunf* (aniseed)
1 tsp coriander powder
10 tsp bread crumbs
Salt to taste
Maida (refined flour) for coating and oil for frying

SHAMI KEBAB

• *Servings 6 persons* • *Preparation time 20 mins.* • *Cooking time 20 mins.*

- Squeeze boiled soya granules thoroughly. Add *channa dal*, onion, green chillies, coriander leaves, red chilli powder, roasted ground *jeera*, *amchur*, *saunf*, coriander powder, bread crumbs and salt.
- Mix all the ingredients and mash them (with hands) till smooth like dough.
- With wet hands, take a small portion of the mixture and make a round ball. Lightly press it and shape it like a *kebab*. Similarly prepare all the *kebabs*.
- Coat each *kebab* with *maida* and dust it. Fry it in hot oil till nicely golden brown.
- Serve hot with curd mixed in mint chutney. Garnish with onion rings and mint leaves.

Ingredients

400 gms *paneer*
1 small finely chopped onion
½ tsp red chilli powder
½ tsp roasted ground *jeera* (cumin seeds)
1 tsp thickly grated ginger
1 clove of garlic (crushed)
½ tsp *amchur* (mango powder)
2 green chillies
4 tsp chopped coriander leaves
4 tsp *maida* (refined flour)
1 tsp salt
Maida and *suji* (semolina) for coating
Oil for shallow frying

Contd.

PANEER KEBAB

• *Servings 6 persons* • *Preparation time 25 mins.* • *Cooking time 15 mins.*

- Mix all the ingredients of the filling — chopped nuts, green chillies, coriander leaves, *jeera, malai* or curd, salt and *paneer* together and keep aside.

PROCEDURE

- Grate *paneer*. Add onion, red chilli powder, *jeera*, ginger, garlic, *amchur*, green chillies, coriander leaves, *maida* and salt. Thoroughly mix them till smooth.
- Divide the mixture into 15 portions. Take each portion and make a round ball.
- Flatten it. Put some filling in the centre, seal it and shape it like a *kebab*.
- Spread some *maida* and *suji* in a plate. Roll each *kebab* in it and dust it.

Contd.

Filling

½ cup chopped nuts and raisins
2 chopped green chillies
2 tsp chopped coriander leaves
½ tsp roasted ground *jeera* (cumin seeds)
2 tsp *malai* or curd
¼ tsp salt
4 tsp grated *paneer* (cottage cheese)

- Similarly make all the *kebabs*.
- Heat oil in a flat pan and fry the *kebabs* till nicely golden brown on both sides.
- Serve hot with mango chutney and potato and pea salad.

Ingredients

1 cup cooked fresh corns or 1 cup corn kernels
1 small finely chopped onion
2 chopped green chillies
1 tsp grated ginger
½ tsp grated garlic
1 medium size boiled potato (grated)
½ cup boiled and mashed peas
4 tsp bread crumbs
4 tsp roasted *besan* (gram flour)
½ tsp ground *jeera* (cumin seeds)
½ tsp *amchur* (mango powder)

Contd.

BHUTTA KEBAB

• *Servings 10 persons* • *Preparation time 25 mins.* • *Cooking time 20 mins.*

- Lightly crush corn kernels with the rolling pin (*belan*). Mix together crushed corns, grated potato, chopped onion, ginger, garlic, green chillies, coriander leaves, bread crumbs, roasted *besan*, *jeera*, *amchur* and salt till smooth like a dough.
- Mix peas, nuts and raisins for filling.
- Divide the mixture into ten portions. Make round balls with each portion and flatten them.
- Put some filling in each and seal it to make a round ball. Flatten it in shape to make into a *kebab*.
- Heat a little oil on a flat pan or *tava*.
- Shallow fry the *kebabs* on both the sides till nicely golden brown and crisp on both the sides.

Contd.

1 tsp salt
Oil for shallow frying
Few nuts and raisins
Chopped coriander leaves

Dhaba Salad
2 medium size onions, cut into thin round slices
¼ tsp salt
¼ tsp red chilli powder
2 tsp coriander leaves
3 tsp lemon juice

Serve hot with Dhaba salad, mint chutney and cucumber and tomato slices.

DHABA SALAD

Mix all the ingredients for the Dhaba salad and serve.

Kebab-e-Mumtaz

Overleaf Bhutta Kebab

BHARWAN KEBAB

Ingredients

8 to 10 medium size boiled potatoes
1 tsp salt
½ tsp turmeric powder
½ tsp red chilli powder
1 tsp coriander powder
½ tsp *ajwain* (caraway seeds)
½ tsp *kasuri methi*
½ tsp roasted ground *jeera* (cumin seeds)
4 tsp lemon juice
3 tsp oil and ½ tsp sugar
A few roasted sesame seeds

Contd.

• *Servings 8 persons* • *Preparation time 30 mins.* • *Baking time 10 mins.*

- Peel potatoes and cut them lengthwise. Scoop out potatoes leaving ½" boundary.
- In a bowl mix together salt, turmeric, red chilli powder, coriander powder, *ajwain, kasuri methi, jeera,* lemon juice, oil and sugar.
- Rub this mixture inside and outside the potato cases and keep them aside for 20 minutes.
- Mix all the ingredients for the filling — grated *paneer,* chopped onion, salt, grated ginger, lemon juice, *malai,* coriander leaves, nuts and raisins together and keep aside.
- Bake the potato cases in a pre-heated oven at 250°C for 8 to 10 minutes till golden brown and crisp.

Contd.

Filling
1 cup grated *paneer*
2 tsp chopped onion
½ tsp salt
1 tsp grated ginger
1 tsp lemon juice
1 tsp *malai* (cream)
2 tsp chopped coriander leaves
A few nuts and raisins chopped

Topping
½ cup crushed cornflakes
A few corieander leaves
Tomato ketchup

- Stuff the potatoes with the prepared filling.
- Sprinkle roasted sesame seeds and crushed cornflakes on top.
- Bake them in a pre-heated oven at 200°C for five minutes.
- Arrange stuffed *kebabs* on a cabbage and carrot bed.
- Sprinkle ketchup and coriander leaves.

Ingredients

½ kg *kamal kakri* (lotus stems)
1 tsp salt
1 tsp red chilli powder
2 tsp coriander powder
1 tsp *anardana* (ground pomegranate seeds)
½ tsp *amchur* (mango powder)
½ tsp *garam masala*
½ tsp *kasuri methi*
2 tsp lemon juice
1 tsp castor sugar
½ tsp crushed garlic (optional)
3 or 4 tsp oil
2 tsp *besan* (gram flour)

Contd.

KAMAL KAKRI KE KEBAB

• *Servings 6 persons* • *Preparation time 30 mins.* • *Cooking time 20 mins.*

- Peel *kamal kakri* and wash them thoroughly. Cut them into 4" pieces.
- Parboil these in salted water. Pass through a sieve and cool them. Pat them dry.
- Beat each piece with a rolling pin.
- Rub salt, red chilli powder, coriander powder, *anardana*, *amchur*, *garam masala*, *kasuri methi*, lemon juice and castor sugar on *kamal kakri*. Keep these covered for 20 minutes.
- Heat oil in a broad pan. Add garlic. Stir and add *besan*. Cook on slow fire for half a minute.
- Add *masala*-coated *kamal kakri*. Cook on high flame for two minutes. Cover with a lid and cook on slow fire for

Contd.

A few green chillies, chopped lengthwise
A few ginger strips
A few coriander leaves

eight minutes. Stir twice in between. Remove the lid and cook on high flame for one or two minutes till crisp and golden brown.

- Garnish with ginger strips, green chillies and coriander leaves.
- Serve hot with sweet tamarind chutney.

RESHMI KEBAB

Ingredients

½ kg *paneer*
½ tsp crushed garlic
1 tsp grated ginger
½ tsp *ajwain* caraway seeds
1½ tsp coriander powder
3 or 4 green chillies, crushed or finely chopped
4 tsp finely chopped coriander leaves
4 tsp hung curd
4 tsp fresh *malai* or cream
2 tsp oil, ½ tsp sugar
A few mint leaves, chopped, A pinch of cardamom powder
Salt to taste (1 tsp)
Tomato ketchup, A lemon or lemon juice
Coriander leaves

- *Servings 6 persons*
- *Preparation time 15 mins. + marination time*
- *Baking time 12 mins.*

- Wash *paneer* and cut it into 1" cubes.
- Keep the cubes in the fridge for half an hour so that they are firm and the water is separated from *paneer*. Drain the water from the *paneer* cubes.
- Marinate the *paneer* pieces with salt, garlic, ginger, coriander powder, *ajwain*, green chillies, coriander leaves, mint leaves, hung curd, *malai* and cardamom powder for half an hour.
- Add oil and sugar and mix them.
- Bake *paneer* pieces in a pre-heated oven at 200°C for 12 minutes till lightly golden brown.
- Sprinkle lemon juice, a little tomato ketchup and coriander leaves.
- Serve with barbecue sauce and salad.

MATTAR KEBAB

Ingredients
2 cups boiled peas (*mattar*)
1 finely chopped small onion
2 or 3 finely chopped green chillies
4 tsp chopped coriander leaves
½ cup boiled *channa dal* (gram lentil)
1 tsp salt
½ tsp roasted ground *jeera* (cumin seeds)
½ tsp *amchur* (mango powder)
½ cup sesame seeds (white) for coating
Chopped mint leaves
A pinch of *garam masala*
Oil for frying

• *Servings 12 persons* • *Preparation time 15 mins.* • *Baking time 15 mins.*

- Lightly mash the peas with your hand. Add onion, green chillies, coriander leaves, mint leaves, boiled *channa dal*, *jeera*, *amchur*, *garam masala* and salt. Thoroughly mix them till smooth like a dough.
- Divide the mixture into 12 portions. Make round balls and flatten them. Shape them like *kebabs*. Coat them with sesame seeds. Shallow fry them in hot oil till golden brown on both the sides. Or sprinkle a little oil and bake in a pre-heated oven at 220°C for 15 minutes.
- Serve hot with cucumber and tomato salad or with sweet mango chutney.

Ingredients

1 medium size boiled beetroot
1 cup boiled *channa dal* (gram lentil)
½ cup grated *paneer*
1 boiled potato, thickly grated
2 finely chopped green chillies
1 tsp thickly grated ginger
½ tsp red chilli powder
1 cup fresh bread crumbs (5 bread slices chopped and churned)
1 tsp coriander powder
½ tsp *kasuri methi*
2 drops of red colour
Oil for frying
Salt to taste (1 tsp)
Suji (semolina) or dry bread crumbs for coating

LAL KEBAB

• *Servings 7 persons* • *Preparation time 25 mins.* • *Cooking time 25 mins.*

- Peel and grate boiled beetroot. Add *channa dal, paneer,* grated potato, green chillies, ginger, fresh bread crumbs, salt, red chilli powder, coriander powder and *kasuri methi*. Mix thoroughly till smooth.
- Divide the mixture into 15 portions. Now take one portion and make an oval shaped *kebab*. Similarly make all the *kebabs*.
- In a separate plate spread some *suji*. Mix two drops of red colour till *suji* looks red in colour.
- Roll each *kebab* in *suji* and dust them.
- Fry them lightly in hot oil and place them on a tissue paper or brown paper.
- Serve hot with tomato and radish salad or tomato chutney.

TILWALE KEBAB

Ingredients
4 medium size boiled potatoes
½ cup finely chopped boiled beans
½ cup corn kernels (cooked corns)
1 thickly grated carrot
4 tsp chopped onion
2 chopped green chillies
4 tsp chopped coriander leaves
¼ tsp crushed garlic
½ tsp grated ginger
6 tsp bread crumbs
1 tsp salt
½ cup crushed cornflakes
1 cup sesame seeds (white)
2 or 3 tsp oil

• *Servings 6 persons* • *Preparation time 20 mins.* • *Baking time 12 mins.*

- Grate potatoes. Add boiled beans, corn, carrot, chopped onion, green chillies, coriander leaves, ginger, garlic, bread crumbs and salt. Mix thoroughly till smooth.
- Make lemon size balls with wet hands out of the mixture.
- In a big flat plate, mix together sesame seeds and crushed cornflakes.
- Roll each *kebab* in sesame seeds and cornflakes mixture and keep aside.
- Bake them in a pre-heated oven at 220°C for 12 minutes till nicely golden brown and crisp (sprinkle a little oil on *kebabs* before baking).
- Serve hot with tomato ketchup and garlic chilli sauce.

Ingredients

4 medium size grated boiled potatoes
1 cup boiled *channa dal* (gram lentil)
1 onion finely chopped
½ tsp red chilli powder
1 tsp coriander powder
1 tsp roasted ground *jeera*
½ cup desiccated coconut or fresh coconut
½ cup grated *paneer*
1 cupful fresh bread crumbs (5 slices crushed)
½ tsp roasted *kalonji*
1 tsp salt
3 tsp lemon juice
½ cup mint chutney
½ cup bread crumbs (dry)
A few curry leaves (chopped)
Refined flour for coating
Oil for frying
Chopped nuts and raisins

PERSIAN KEBAB

• *Servings 6 persons* • *Preparation time 30 mins.* • *Cooking time 20 mins.*

- In a large bowl, mix together potatoes, *channa dal*, *paneer*, desiccated coconut, onion, red chilli powder, coriander powder, roasted ground *jeera*, chopped nuts and raisins, fresh bread crumbs, curry leaves, *kalonji*, salt and lemon juice. Mix till smooth.
- Take a small portion of the mixture. Make a round ball and press it. Similarly make balls with the rest of the mixture.
- Coat each ball with flour and dust it. Now roll them in mint chutney and coat with bread crumbs.
- Fry them in hot oil till nicely golden brown.
- Garnish with onion rings and mint leaves.
- Serve with sweet mint chutney with nuts.

Ingredients
10 medium size mushrooms
10 1" pieces of *paneer* (cottage cheese)
10 small baby corns
10 big diced pieces of onion
10 big diced pieces of capsicum
5 pineapple slices chopped into broad pieces
½ tsp red chilli powder
½ tsp crushed garlic
1 tsp salt

Contd.

MEXICAN KEBAB

- *Servings 5 persons*
- *Preparation time 15 mins. + marination time*
- *Baking time 15 mins.*

- Mix salt, red chilli powder, crushed garlic, oregano, Tobasco sauce, a pinch of *kesar*, hung curd, lemon juice, sugar and olive oil in a small bowl for marination.
- Now marinate *paneer*, mushrooms, baby corns, onion, capsicum and pineapple pieces with the prepared marinade. Keep them in the refrigerator for an hour.
- Grease five skewers and thread the marinated vegetables.
- First of all thread *paneer*, then onion, baby corn, capsicum, and a pineapple piece. Repeat the same pattern again on the same skewer.
- Similarly arrange rest of the four skewers.
- Either roast them on charcoal *sigri* or bake them in a pre-heated oven at 220°C for 15 minutes.

Contd.

½ tsp oregano
1 tsp Tobasco sauce
4 tsp hung curd
2 tsp lemon juice
1 tsp sugar
2 tsp olive oil
A pinch of *kesar* (saffron)

- Sprinkle lemon juice and chilli flakes.
- Serve them on a bed of *kesar* rice with lots of lettuce leaves.

STUFFED CAPSICUM KEBAB

Ingredients
12 small size capsicums

Filling
3 tsp oil
1 finely chopped small onion
6 tsp *besan* (gram flour)
1 tsp red chilli powder
1 tsp *amchur* (mango powder)
2 tsp coriander powder
1 tsp grated ginger
1 tsp roasted ground *jeera* (cumin seeds)
½ tsp sugar
2 tsp lemon juice
½ tsp *kasuri methi*
1 tsp salt + 4 tsp chopped nuts
A clove of garlic
Coriander leaves
Beaten curd

• *Servings 6 persons* • *Preparation time 20 mins.* • *Baking time 10 mins.*

- Wash capsicums and wipe them. Cut a thin slice from the top and remove the seeds and the stalk and keep aside.

FILLING

- Heat oil, add onion and cook for half a minute. Add *besan* and sauté for a minute. Mix red chilli powder, coriander powder, *jeera, amchur* and *kasuri methi*. Cook for a minute on slow fire. Add ginger, garlic, salt and sugar and mix them. Add lemon juice and nuts; remove from the fire and cool this mixture.
- Fill 1 tsp filling in each capsicum. Brush them with oil.
- Bake (roast) them in a pre-heated oven at 220°C for 10 minutes till the capsicums are crisp and tender. Garnish with onion rings and coriander leaves.
- Sprinkle beaten curd on top. Serve with crisp potato wafers.

Ingredients

2 cups boiled black *channa* (black chickpeas)
1 small finely chopped onion
2 finely chopped green chillies
4 tsp chopped coriander leaves
½ cup bread crumbs
2 tsp lemon juice
1 tsp crushed garlic
1 tsp grated ginger
½ tsp red chilli powder
1 tsp coriander powder
½ tsp *garam masala*
½ cup grated *paneer*
1 medium size boiled potato (grated)

Contd.

CHANNA KEBAB

• *Servings 15 persons* • *Preparation time 25 mins.*
• *Baking or frying time 12 mins.*

- Lightly blend together boiled black *channa*, ginger, garlic, red chilli powder, coriander powder, *garam masala*, *paneer* and potato.
- Add onion, green chillies, coriander leaves, bread crumbs, salt and lemon juice. Mix thoroughly till smooth.
- Divide the mixture into 15 portions. With wet hands make round balls of each portion and lightly press them like *kebabs*.
- Mix together bread crumbs and crushed cornflakes and roll each *kebab* in it. Sprinkle a little oil on them.
- Bake them in a pre-heated oven at 200°C for 12 minutes till golden brown or crisp.

Contd.

Salt to taste (1 tsp)
Bread crumbs and crushed cornflakes for coating

VARIATION

- You can fry them in hot oil till nicely golden brown.
- Serve hot with garlic and mango chutney or with onion rings and lemon wedges.

PUDINA-AALU KEBAB

Ingredients
12 boiled baby potatoes
3 tsp oil
½ tsp crushed garlic
1 tsp grated ginger
3 or 4 green chillies, very finely chopped
3 tsp lemon juice
½ tsp sugar
1 tsp roasted ground *jeera* (cumin seeds)
¼ tsp black rock salt
½ cup chopped mint leaves

• *Servings 6 persons* • *Preparation time 15 mins.* • *Cooking time 10 mins.*

- Peel potatoes and thoroughly prick them. Rub black rock salt, ginger, garlic, lemon juice and sugar over them. Keep them covered for 15 minutes.
- Now heat oil in a pan till smoky hot. Add potatoes and stir fry for five minutes till dry and light golden brown in colour.
- Add chopped mint leaves, green chillies and roasted ground *jeera*. Again cook for a minute.
- Remove from fire. Sprinkle barbecue *masala*.
- Serve them with cocktail drinks or mocktails.

Ingredients
½ cup blanched peas
1 cup boiled *channa dal* (gram lentil)
½ cup grated coconut
1 small finely chopped onion
2 chopped green chillies
½ tsp red chilli powder
½ tsp *garam masala*
½ tsp *amchur* (mango powder)
½ tsp crushed garlic
1 tsp grated ginger
5 or 6 tsp roasted *besan* (gram flour)
1 tsp salt
2 tsp *khus khus* (poppy seeds)
Oil for frying
Chopped coriander leaves

SEEKH KEBAB

• *Servings 6 persons* • *Preparation time 15 mins.* • *Cooking time 20 mins.*

- Mix together *channa dal*, grated coconut, peas, onion, green chillies, coriander leaves, red chilli powder, *garam masala*, *amchur*, ginger, garlic, roasted *besan*, salt and *khus-khus* together till smooth.
- Grease the wooden skewer (*seekh*) and roll and spread a small portion of the mixture. Similarly prepare all other *seekhs*. Fry the mixture in hot oil till nicely golden brown. Carefully remove the *seekhs* from the skewers.
- Serve them with *pyaaz ka lachcha* (onion rings), green chillies and lemon wedges.
- You can roast them under the grill. Sprinkle a little oil on the *seekh* before roasting.

Kamal Kakri ke Kebab ➤
Overleaf Tilwale Kebab

SATRANGA KEBAB

Ingredients
10 pieces of diced capsicum
10 pieces of *paneer* ½" thick and 2" square
10 pieces of carrot diced broad
10 pieces of diced onion
10 pieces of diced pineapple
10 pieces of diced beetroot
10 pieces of yellow capsicum or red capsicum
½ cup bread crumbs for coating

Marinade
1½ tsp salt + 2 tsp honey
1 tsp red chilli powder
3 tsp lemon juice
1 tsp crushed garlic
1 tsp finely grated ginger
½ tsp roasted ground *jeera* (cumin seeds)
2 tsp oil
½ tsp sugar + 2 tsp vinegar

• *Servings 10 persons* • *Preparation time 20 mins.* • *Baking time 15 mins.*

- In a cup mix all the ingredients for marinade.
- Pour this on the diced vegetables and thoroughly mix them.
- Keep covered in the fridge for an hour.
- Arrange one over another; a piece of capsicum, then carrot, onion, *paneer*, pineapple, beetroot and yellow capsicum.
- Press them and coat with bread crumbs.
- Fix one toothpick in the centre. Keep aside.
- Similarly prepare the other *kebabs*.
- Roast them in a pre-heated oven at 200°C for 15 minutes till nicely golden brown and crisp.
- Remove the toothpick and sprinkle lemon juice.
- Serve hot with finger fries and Dhaba salad.

KATHAL (JACKFRUIT) KEBAB

Ingredients

½ kg *kathal* (jackfruit without skin) 1" pieces
½ cup hung curd
1 tsp salt
1 tsp red chilli powder
2 tsp coriander powder
½ tsp *garam masala*
¼ tsp cardamom powder
1 tsp mint paste
1 tsp ginger paste
4 or 5 tsp *maida* (refined flour)
Oil for frying
A pinch of orange colour
Half lemon juice (2 tsp)
4 tsp sesame seeds
1 tsp garlic paste
Chaat masala

• *Servings 6 persons* • *Preparation time 10 mins. + marination time 1 hour*
• *Cooking time 15 mins. + 5 mins. baking*

- Pressure cook *kathal* for half a minute with water, oil and salt. Pass this through a sieve and cool. Pat dry.
- Prick *kathal* lightly. Marinate it with salt, red chilli powder, coriander powder, *garam masala*, cardamom powder, mint paste, garlic paste, ginger paste, hung curd and orange colour for an hour.
- Add *maida* and sesame seeds to the marinated *kathal*. Thoroughly mix them so that *kathal* is coated with *maida* and sesame seeds.
- Heat oil and fry the coated *kathal* till light golden brown.
- Sprinkle lemon juice and *chaat masala* and grill the *kathal* in a pre-heated oven for five minutes at 250°C, till crisp and nicely golden brown.
- Serve hot with *roomali roti* and tomato chutney.

TANDOORI KHUMBI

Ingredients

2 packets of mushrooms (400 gms)
4 tsp hung curd
3 tsp lemon juice
1 tsp salt
½ tsp red chilli powder
1 tsp coriander powder
1 tsp crushed garlic
1 tsp grated ginger
2 green chillies, finely chopped
4 tsp chopped coriander leaves
1 pinch of *hing* (asafoetida)
½ tsp sugar
2 tsp oil
4 tsp bread crumbs
2 tsp roasted *besan* (gram flour)
Chaat masala

- *Servings 6 persons*
- *Preparation time 15 mins. + marination time*
- *Baking time 13 mins.*

- Wash mushrooms and pat them dry. Prick the cap (round part). Now mix together hung curd, lemon juice, red chilli powder, coriander powder, crushed garlic, ginger, green chillies, coriander leaves, asafoetida, salt, oil and sugar till smooth. Now marinate the mushrooms thoroughly. Keep aside for half an hour.
- Mix bread crumbs and roasted *besan* into marinated mushrooms. Now roast them in a pre-heated oven at 200°C for 13 minutes till brown and crisp.
- Sprinkle *chaat masala* and then lemon juice. Serve with onion rings and sweet and sour chutney.
- Sweet and sour chutney can be made by mixing together mint chutney, ketchup and cream in equal quantity.

Ingredients
400 gms small *baigun* (brinjals)
6 boiled small potatoes
Masala
1 tsp salt
2 tsp coriander powder
½ tsp *garam masala*
1 tsp red chilli powder
1 tsp roasted ground *jeera* (cumin seeds)
¼ tsp turmeric powder
1 tsp *anardana* (dry pomegranate seeds)
½ tsp *amchur* (mango powder)
½ tsp *kasuri methi*
½ tsp castor sugar + 3 tsp oil
4 tsp melon seeds (ground) (*magaz*)
Ginger juliennes

TANDOORI BAIGUN

• *Servings 6 persons* • *Preparation time 20 mins.*
• *Roasting time 17 mins.*

- Mix together salt, coriander powder, red chilli powder, roasted ground *jeera*, turmeric powder, *anardana*, *amchur*, *kasuri methi*, castor sugar and crushed melon seeds.
- Make slits in *baigun* and potatoes. Fill the *masala* in them. Sprinkle oil and lightly mix them.
- Roast them in a pre-heated oven at 200°C for 15 minutes.
- Sprinkle beaten curd and *garam masala* on them and again bake for two minutes.
- Serve hot with ginger juliennes or onion rings.

Ingredients
15 to 20 parboiled baby potatoes

Marinade
1 tsp salt
½ tsp red chilli powder
⅓ tsp turmeric powder
½ tsp garlic paste
½ tsp roasted and ground *jeera* (cumin seeds)
½ tsp *ajwain* (caraway seeds)
4 tsp lemon juice
3 tsp oil
½ tsp sugar

Contd.

BARBECUE POTATOES

• *Servings 6 persons* • *Preparation time ½ hour*
• *Cooking time 5 mins. + Baking time 12 mins.*

- Peel potatoes and lightly prick them.
- Mix all the ingredients of marinade and lightly rub the marinade on the potatoes and keep aside for 15 minutes.

FILLING

- Melt butter, add *besan* and cook for half a minute.
- Add onion, green chillies, coriander leaves, chopped cashewnuts, ginger, *jeera* and salt.
- Cook for half a minute. Mix lemon juice and remove from fire. Cool the mixture.
- Roast (bake) the potatoes in a pre-heated oven at 200°C for 12 minutes till crisp and golden brown.

Contd.

Filling
4 tsp finely chopped onion
2 green chillies finely chopped
4 tsp chopped coriander leaves
15 to 20 finely chopped cashewnuts
1 tsp grated ginger
1 tsp lemon juice
1 tsp butter
1 tsp *besan* (gram flour)
¼ tsp salt
¼ tsp *jeera* (cumin seeds)
Grated carrot
Boiled peas

- Scoop out a small piece from the centre of each potato.
- Fill it with a little filling and cover the scooped out piece of potato on top. Fix one toothpick deep into it.
- Serve potatoes on a cabbage bed.
- Sprinkle lemon juice.
- Garnish with grated carrot and boiled peas.

Ingredients
½ kg *paneer,* chopped into 1" cubes
Onion rings
Mint chutney
Roomali roti

Marinade
1 tsp salt
1 tsp red chilli powder
2 tsp coriander powder
½ tsp *ajwain* (caraway seeds)
½ tsp *garam masala*
½ tsp *kasuri methi*
4 tsp lemon juice
½ tsp sugar
3 tsp oil
4 tsp roasted *besan* (gram flour)
2 tsp *chaat masala*

TANDOORI PANEER

• *Servings 6 persons* • *Preparation time 10 mins. + marination time* • *Roasting time 6 mins.*

- Marinate *paneer* pieces in salt, red chilli powder, coriander powder, *ajwain*, *garam masala*, *kasuri methi*, lemon juice, oil and sugar for half an hour. Now sprinkle *besan* on the *paneer* pieces. Thread them in skewers.
- Pre-heat the *tandoor* for four minutes. Arrange the skewers in the *tandoor* and roast for six minutes. After three minutes change the side.
- Sprinkle *chaat masala* on *tandoori paneer* and squeeze lemon juice.
- Serve hot with onion rings, mint chutney and *roomali roti*.

NUTRELLA TIKKA

Ingredients

100 gms soya chunks (Ruchi/Nutrella cubes)
½ cup curd
½ tsp crushed garlic
1½ tsp grated ginger
1 tsp salt
2 tsp coriander powder
½ tsp *ajwain* (caraway seeds)
2 tsp lemon juice
2 green chillies
2 tsp chopped coriander leaves
3 tsp oil
½ tsp sugar
4 to 5 cloves
A cinnamon stick
A pinch of orange colour

• Servings 10 persons • Boiling time 5 mins. + marination time
• Cooking time 10 mins. + Baking time 5 mins.

- Wash Nutrella chunks.
- Boil water along with ¼ tsp salt. Add washed chunks of Nutrella and boil for five minutes. Pass it through a sieve and cool them.
- Squeeze Nutrella chunks. Marinate them with ginger, garlic, salt, coriander powder, *ajwain*, lemon juice, green chillies, coriander leaves, curd and orange colour. Thoroughly mix them and keep for half an hour.
- Heat oil in a pan, add cloves, cinnamon, stir and add marinated Nutrella. Cook on high flame till dry and brown. Add 4 tsp water and sugar. Cook till dry.
- Grill them in a pre-heated oven at 200°C for five minutes.
- Sprinkle lemon juice. Serve with onion rings and mint chutney.

Ingredients
1 cup *aata* (wheat flour)
1 cup *maida* (refined flour)
½ tsp salt
2 tsp oil
Lukewarm water for kneading the dough
Oil for cooking rolls
A few onion *lachcha*
6 tsp mint chutney

Filling
400 gms *paneer*
1 tsp salt
1 tsp red chilli powder
½ tsp *ajwain* (caraway seeds)
½ tsp *kasuri methi*
3 tsp lemon juice
½ tsp crushed garlic
1 tsp grated ginger
2 tsp oil

KATHI ROLLS

• *Servings 6 persons* • *Preparation time 15 mins. + marination time* • *Cooking time 15 mins.*

- Sieve *aata, maida* and salt together. Add oil and mix well. Now gradually add water and make a soft and smooth dough. Keep aside for half an hour.
- Cut *paneer* into 1" cubes. Rub salt, red chilli powder, *ajwain, kasuri methi,* lemon juice, ginger, garlic and oil. Refrigerate for half an hour.
- Grease the skewers (thin iron rods) and thread *paneer*. Grill them in pre-heated oven for 10 minutes at 200°C, till crisp and golden brown.
- Roll *chappati* of 8"-diameter from the prepared dough. Cook on pre-heated *tava* (griddle). Spread a little oil on both the sides and cook till crisp.
- Arrange roasted *paneer,* onion *lachcha* and mint chutney in the *chappati* and roll it. Fix one toothpick in it.
- Serve hot with cucumber-tomato salad and lemon wedges.

ADRAKI GOBHI TIKKA

Ingredients
1 kg *gobhi* (cauliflower)
1½ tsp salt
1 tsp red chilli powder
2 tsp coriander powder
¼ tsp turmeric powder
½ tsp *garam masala*
½ tsp *kasuri methi*
1 tsp roasted ground *jeera* (cumin seeds)
1 tsp *saunf* (ground aniseed)
2 tsp finely grated *adrak* (ginger)
6 tsp lemon juice
3 tsp cream or *malai*
3 tsp oil + ½ tsp sugar
A drop of orange colour (optional)

- *Servings 8 persons* • *Preparation time 20 mins.* • *Baking time 15 mins.*

- Remove the stalk and leaves from the cauliflower. Cut big and broad pieces out of it.
- In a big vessel boil enough water with ½ tsp salt. Add cauliflower. Cover with a lid and switch off the gas. Keep covered for five minutes and pass through a sieve. Cool it.
- Marinate cauliflower with all the ingredients, i.e. salt, red chilli powder, coriander powder, turmeric powder, *garam masala*, *kasuri methi*, *jeera*, *saunf*, ginger, lemon juice, cream, oil, sugar and orange colour for 30 minutes.
- Roast cauliflower in a pre-heated oven at 220°C for 15 minutes till it is crisp and golden brown.
- Sprinkle lemon juice.
- Serve on a bed of yellow rice and onions in vinegar or with cucumber and radish salad.

TAVA AALU, ARVI, KAMAL KAKRI

• *Servings 8 persons* • *Preparation time 20 mins.* • *Cooking time 10 mins.*

Ingredients

6 to 8 boiled baby potatoes
6 to 8 parboiled *arvi* (colocasia)
300 gms *kamal kakri* (lotus stems), chopped into 3" pieces and boiled
3 chopped tomatoes

Masala

1½ tsp salt
1 tsp red chilli powder
3 tsp coriander powder
1½ *amchur* or *anardana*
½ tsp turmeric powder
1½ tsp *kasuri methi*
1 tsp *garam masala*
6 tsp *besan*, 4 tsp oil
½ tsp *kalonji* (onion seeds)
½ tsp mustard seeds
½ tsp sugar
4 or 5 green chillies, sliced
A few strips of ginger

- Heat oil, add *kalonji* and mustard seeds. Cook till the seeds crackle. Add *besan* and cook for a minute (on slow fire). Now add red chilli powder, coriander powder, *anardana*, turmeric powder, *kasuri methi* and *garam masala*. Cook for half a minute. Mix in salt and sugar. Remove from fire and cool it.
- Make a slit (lengthwise) in the potatoes, *arvi* and *kamal kakri*.
- Fill the roasted *masala* in them. Heat a little oil in a flat pan or *tava*. Put *aalu*, *arvi* and *kamal kakri* and saute for two or three minutes. Sprinkle left over *masala*, ginger, tomatoes and green chillies. Cover and cook for eight minutes. Remove the lid and again saute till crisp and dry. Sprinkle lemon juice and a little salt or butter.
- Serve hot with *tandoori roti* or *naan*.

SHASHLIK VEGETABLES ON SAFFRON RICE

Ingredients

1 cup long grain rice
3 tsp oil
½ tsp *kesar* (saffron) soaked in 2 tsp water
3 or 4 crushed cardamoms
3 or 4 cloves
1 stick of cinnamon
1 tsp salt
2 cups water

Shashlik Vegetables

2 onions, diced
1 carrot, diced
1 capsicum, diced
8 to 10 mushrooms
8 to 10 1" cubes of *paneer*
1 tsp salt
1 tsp red chilli powder
1 tsp *garam masala*
1 tsp crushed garlic
3 tsp lemon juice
3 tsp oil + ½ tsp sugar
½ tsp barbecue *masala*

• *Servings 6 persons* • *Preparation time 15 mins.*
• *Cooking time 15 mins. + roasting time 12 mins.*

- Wash the rice thoroughly and soak for 15 minutes.
- Heat oil, add cloves, cardamom and cinnamon. Cook till they crackle.
- Add rice and cook till crisp and dry.
- Add water and cook till the rice boils.
- Add salt and *kesar* (saffron).
- Cover and cook till rice is tender. Lightly stir it.
- Marinate the vegetables with salt, red chilli powder, *garam masala*, barbecue *masala*, lemon juice, garlic, oil and sugar for an hour.
- Thread them on a skewer, along with *paneer* cubes.
- Roast in a pre-heated oven at 220°C till golden brown.
- Sprinkle lemon juice. Garnish with cucumber and tomato salad.
- Serve on the *kesar* rice bed.

KASHMIRI TIKKA

Ingredients
½ kg *paneer*

Marinade
6 tsp hung curd
1 tsp salt
½ tsp *Kashmiri mirch* (red pepper)
¼ tsp turmeric powder
2 tsp finely grated ginger
1 tsp crushed garlic
¼ tsp *kesar* (saffron)
¼ tsp cardamom powder
½ tsp *saunf* (ground aniseed)
½ tsp *kasuri methi*
4 tsp ground cashewnut
½ tsp sugar
3 tsp oil
1 stick of cinnamon

- *Servings 6 persons* • *Preparation time 25 mins.*
- *Cooking time 10 mins. + Baking time 5 mins.*

- Wash *paneer* and cut it into 1½" cubes. Keep this in the fridge for 30 minutes. Keep on a strainer for five minutes.
- Mix together hung curd, *Kashmiri mirch*, turmeric powder, *kasuri methi, saunf,* cardamom powder, ginger, garlic, salt and sugar till smooth.
- Marinate *paneer* pieces with the prepared marinade. Keep aside for half an hour. Sprinkle *kesar*.
- Heat oil in a pan till smoky hot. Add cinnamon and stir it. Add marinated *paneer*. Cook on a high flame till slightly brown and dry. Now coat *paneer* with ground cashewnuts.
- Grill *paneer* in a pre-heated oven at 200°C till golden brown. Sprinkle lemon juice. Serve with sweet tomato chutney or dates chutney.

Ingredients
6 *kathi* wraps
6 tsp mint chutney
2 cup boiled chickpeas
2 potatoes, boiled and chopped into 1" pieces
100 gms *paneer* as 1" cubes
1 diced onion
1 diced tomato
1" piece of ginger chopped into slices
2 green chillies sliced lengthwise
1 tsp red chilli powder
2 tsp coriander powder
½ tsp *kasuri methi*
½ tsp *garam masala*
1 tsp *anardana*
1 tsp *amchur* + ½ tsp *saunf*
1 tsp roasted ground *jeera*
½ tsp lemon juice
½ tsp sugar
1 tsp salt + 4 tsp oil

PINDI KEBAB ROLL

- *Servings 6 persons*
- *Preparation time 15 mins. + marination time*
- *Cooking time 15 mins.*

- Marinate chickpeas, potato cubes, *paneer*, onion and tomato with salt, red chilli powder, coriander powder, *kasuri methi, garam masala, anardana, amchur*, roasted ground *jeera, saunf,* lemon juice and sugar for half an hour.
- Heat oil in a large pan, add ginger, green chillies and cook for half a minute.
- Add marinated chickpeas, potatoes, *paneer*, onion and tomatoes. Cook on a high flame for five minutes till dry.
- Grill the chickpeas in a pre-heated oven at 200°C for five minutes.
- Divide the chickpeas mixture into six parts.
- Spread chickpeas *kebab, paneer,* potato, onion and tomato mixture in each *kathi* wrap. Sprinkle mint chutney and roll the wrap.
- Serve hot with tomato sauce and *lasunia* chutney along with onion rings.

TANDOORI GOBHI

Ingredients
1 big *gobhi* (cauliflower)
2 boiled potatoes

Marinade
1 tsp red chilli powder
2 tsp crushed garlic
½ cup finely chopped mint leaves
2 tsp finely chopped onion
2 finely chopped green chillies
2 tsp coriander powder
½ cup hung curd
1 tsp salt
½ tsp *garam masala*
¼ tsp cinnamon powder
1 big black cardamom seeds, crushed

Contd.

- *Servings 6 persons*
- *Preparation time 20 mins. + marination time*
- *Baking time 15 mins.*

- Cut thick and broad pieces of cauliflower. Blanch and cool them.
- Cut thick and broad pieces of potatoes.
- Marinate cauliflower and potatoes together with green chillies, red chilli powder, garlic, mint leaves, coriander powder, *garam masala*, cinnamon powder, crushed cardamom seeds, hung curd, salt, sugar and oil for 30 minutes.
- Mix bread crumbs thoroughly.
- Thread cauliflower and potatoes into skewers.
- Roast them in an electric *tandoor* or clay oven or in a pre-heated oven at 220°C for 15 minutes till cauliflower is crisp and brown.
- Sprinkle lemon juice.

Contd.

½ tsp sugar + 3 tsp oil
4 tsp crushed dry bread crumbs
1 cup boiled peas

- Garnish with onion rings and boiled peas.

HOW TO BLANCH

- Boil enough water along with ½ tsp salt. When it starts boiling, add cauliflower. Cover with lid and remove from the fire. Keep for five minutes. Pass through a sieve and cool.

Satranga Kebab ➤
Overleaf Tandoori Baigun

Ingredients
½ tsp *kesar* (saffron)
4 tsp *gulab jal* (rosewater)
25 to 30 cashewnuts
25 to 30 large size, soaked and peeled almonds
25 to 30 raisins
250 gms *paneer* chopped into ½" cubes
25 gms *makhane* (lotus seeds)
6 to 8 tsp cream or fresh *malai*
3 or 4 tsp curd
2 tsp honey
½ tsp coarsely ground black pepper
½ tsp roasted ground *jeera*
¼ tsp cardamom powder
½ tsp salt + 2 tsp oil
Chopped coriander leaves

KESAR-GULAB TIKKA

- *Servings 6 persons* • *Preparation time 25 mins.*
- *Cooking time 5 mins. + Baking time 10 minutes*

- Mix together *kesar, gulab jal, malai,* curd, honey, black pepper, *jeera*, cardamom powder, salt, coriander leaves and oil and keep aside.
- In another bowl arrange cashewnuts, almonds, raisins, *paneer* and *makhane*.
- Mix in the above prepared *kesar-gulab* mixture thoroughly. Keep aside for 15 minutes. Now grease a pan and cook all the ingredients on a high flame till dry.
- Bake them in a pre-heated oven at 200°C for 10 minutes till nicely golden brown. Squeeze lemon juice on them.
- Decorate with silver leaf (*verk*). Garnish with grated *paneer*.
- Serve them on a rose-petal bed.

AFGHANI PANEER TIKKA

Ingredients
½ *kg paneer*
½ cup hung curd
1 tsp salt
3 or 4 crushed green chillies
¼ tsp cardamom powder
1 tsp coriander powder
½ tsp *kasuri methi*
½ tsp garlic paste
½ tsp ginger paste
½ tsp sugar
4 tsp grated cashewnuts
2 tsp oil
Chopped coriander leaves
Lemon juice

- *Servings 6 persons*
- *Preparation time 10 mins. + marination time*
- *Baking time 12 mins.*

- Cut *paneer* into 2" by 1" pieces. Marinate them with hung curd, green chillies, coriander leaves, coriander powder, ginger and garlic paste, *kasuri methi*, salt and sugar. Mix them. Sprinkle cardamom powder. Keep in the refrigerator for 30 minutes.
- In a plate spread grated cashewnuts.
- Coat each piece of marinated *paneer* with cashewnuts. Drizzle oil on them. Bake coated *paneer* in a pre-heated oven at 220°C for 12 minutes, till lightly golden brown.
- Sprinkle lemon juice and coriander leaves. Roll them in *roomali roti*. Fix with a toothpick each.
- Serve them with *pyaaz ka lachcha* (onion rings) and tomato chutney.

Ingredients
12 small size onions
1 tsp salt
½ tsp red chilli powder
3 tsp lemon juice
3 tsp vinegar
1 tsp sugar
½ tsp crushed garlic
1 tsp roasted ground *jeera* (cumin seeds)
3 or 4 green chillies sliced lengthwise
1 capsicum (diced)
2 tomatoes without pulp (diced)
2 or 3 pineapple slices (broad pieces)
3 tsp oil
Few strips of ginger
4 tsp chopped coriander leaves

ONION TIKKA

• *Servings 6 persons* • *Preparation time 10 mins. + marination time 30 mins.*
• *Cooking time 4 mins. + roasting time*

- Peel onions, wash and wipe them. Prick them all over.
- In a bowl mix together onion, capsicum, pineapple pieces and tomatoes. Marinate them with salt, red chilli powder, lemon juice, vinegar, sugar, crushed garlic, roasted ground *jeera* for 30 minutes.
- Heat oil in a pan. Add marinated onions, tomatoes, capsicum and pineapple pieces. Cook for four minutes on a high flame. Remove from fire and mix tomato pieces, ginger strips and green chillies. Sprinkle coriander leaves.
- Thread them in skewers and grill them in a pre-heated oven till crisp and golden brown.
- Serve hot with garlic bread and sour cream.

LACHCHEDAR TIKKA

Ingredients
2 medium or 1 large onion
2 capsicums
1 big carrot
100 gms beans
150 gms *paneer*
1 big boiled potato
2 large tomatoes
2 pineapple slices
1 small cucumber
1 boiled beetroot
3 or 4 green or red chillies
A few ginger strips

Marinade
1 tsp salt
1 tsp red chilli powder
2 tsp coriander powder

Contd.

- *Servings 8 persons* • *Preparation time 30 mins.*
- *Cooking time 10 mins. + roasting time*

- Cut onion into thin round slices. Cut capsicums into long thin strips; chop the carrot into long thin strips; slice beans lengthwise and blanch them.
- Cut potato into thin long fingers, tomatoes into long thin strips. Cut *paneer* into long strips. Slice pineapple into strips; chop beetroot into thin strips; slice cucumber into thin, long slices. Cut green chillies lengthwise and ginger too.
- Marinate all the ingredients except (cucumber and beetroot) with salt, red chilli powder, *ajwain*, crushed garlic, *jeera*, lemon juice, coriander powder, oil and sugar thoroughly.
- Keep aside for 15 minutes.
- Now mix cucumber and beetroot slices.

Contd.

½ tsp *ajwain* (caraway seeds)
½ tsp crushed garlic
1 tsp roasted ground *jeera*
5 tsp lemon juice
½ tsp sugar
2 tsp oil

- Grease a large pan and sauté all the ingredients for four minutes on high flame.
- In a baking dish grill sauted vegetables for 8 to 10 minutes in a pre-heated oven at 220°C.
- Now serve this on a cabbage bed. Sprinkle lemon juice. Garnish with onion rings and mint leaves.

MALAI TIKKA

Ingredients
200 gms mushrooms
250 gms *paneer*
1 tsp salt
4 tsp hung curd
8 tsp fresh *malai* or ⅓ cup cream
½ tsp red chilli powder
1 tsp coriander powder
½ tsp *garam masala*
1 pinch of *kesar* (saffron)
¼ tsp cardamom powder
6 tsp ground cashewnuts
1 tsp oil
A pinch of sugar (¼ tsp)

• *Servings 6 persons* • *Preparation time 25 mins.* • *Baking time 12 mins.*

- Wash and wipe the mushrooms and prick them. Cut *paneer* into 1" cubes and prick them.
- Marinate mushrooms and *paneer* with salt, hung curd, *malai*, red chilli powder, coriander powder, *garam masala*, *kesar*, cardamom powder and sugar for an hour.
- Heat oil, add marinated mushrooms and *paneer* pieces. Cook on high flame till dry. Coat them in ground cashewnut.
- Grill them in a pre-heated oven at 200°C for 10 minutes till golden brown.
- Sprinkle lemon juice and rose-petals. Serve them with mango chutney.

STUFFED MUSHROOM TIKKA

Ingredients
20 button mushrooms
(approximately 400 gms)
Lettuce leaves
Tomato ketchup
Mint leaves

Marinade
1 tsp salt
½ tsp red chilli powder
½ tsp *kasuri methi*
½ tsp crushed garlic
(optional)
2 tsp lemon juice
1 tsp oil

Contd.

• *Servings 6 persons* • *Preparation time 10 mins. + marination time*
• *Cooking time 15 mins.*

- Wash mushrooms and wipe them. Remove the stem as this is not used in this recipe.
- Prick the mushrooms and marinate them with salt, red chilli powder, *kasuri methi*, garlic, lemon juice, oil and sugar for 30 minutes.
- Toss bread crumbs in the marinated mushrooms and bake them in a pre-heated oven at 220°C for 10 minutes.
- Mix all the ingredients of the filling — *paneer*, salt, *jeera*, grated cheese cube, lemon juice, green chilli, coriander leaves, *malai* and nuts.
- In each baked mushroom fill the prepared filling and press it.

Contd.

½ tsp sugar
4 tsp bread crumbs

Filling
100 gms *paneer*
½ tsp salt
½ tsp ground *jeera* (cumin seeds)
1 tsp lemon juice
1 finely chopped green chilli
2 tsp chopped coriander leaves
1 tsp cream or *malai* (milk top)
A few finely chopped nuts
A grated cheese cube (28 gms)

- Again bake them in a pre-heated oven at 200°C for five minutes.
- Arrange some lettuce leaves in a serving dish and then arrange the stuffed mushroom *tikka* on it.
- Garnish with tomato ketchup and mint leaves.
- Serve hot with toast or fried bread and dates chutney.

TANDOORI SALAD

• *Servings 6 persons* • *Preparation time 20 mins.* • *Roasting time 5 mins.*

Ingredients

350 gms *paneer* cut into broad pieces
1 large diced capsicum
2 diced onion
1 diced carrot
3 pineapple slices, chopped into big pieces
2 tomatoes cut in broad pieces

Marinade

1 tsp salt
½ tsp red chilli powder
1 tsp coriander powder
¼ tsp *ajwain* (caraway seeds)
2 or 3 tsp lemon juice
½ tsp crushed garlic
2 tsp oil
½ tsp sugar
A drop of orange colour

- Mix the ingredients of marinade and keep them in two separate bowls. Marinate *paneer* in one and vegetables in the other bowl. Keep aside for half an hour.
- Grill *paneer* in a pre-heated oven at 200°C for eight minutes till marinade is dry or you can roast it in a heated greased pan till dry.
- In a separate greased pan (smoky hot) roast vegetables for four minutes.
- Mix *paneer* pieces in vegetables and cook for a minute.
- Put it in a serving bowl. Sprinkle lemon juice. Garnish with shredded cabbage, onion rings and lemon wedges.

KEBABWALA PARANTHA

Ingredients

1 bowl of assorted leftover *kebabs* or prepared *kebabs*
1 finely chopped onion
2 chopped green chillies
4 tsp coriander leaves
1 tsp *anardana* (dry pomegranate seeds)
1 tsp grated ginger
½ tsp salt

Contd.

• *Servings 6 persons* • *Preparation time 10 mins.* • *Cooking time 30 mins.*

- Sieve *aata, maida, suji* and salt together. Add oil. Mix well. Add water gradually and make a smooth and soft dough. Cover with a wet napkin and keep aside for 30 minutes.
- Chop the *kebabs* into small bits. Mix onion, green chillies, coriander leaves, grated ginger, *anardana* and salt in the *kebabs.*
- Make two lemon size balls and roll them into 6"-diameter *chappatis.*
- On one *chappati* spread about 5 or 6 tsp of the *kebab* filling. Arrange second *chappati* over it. Press the edges and lightly roll it again.
- Cook in a pre-heated or greased *tava* (griddle) on a

Contd.

Dough
1 cup *aata* (wheat flour)
1 cup *suji* (semolina)
1 cup *maida* (refined flour)
½ tsp salt
3 or 4 tsp oil or *ghee*
Lukewarm water for kneading the dough
Ghee or oil for cooking *parantha*

medium flame. Lightly apply *ghee* or oil on both sides to cook the *parantha* golden brown on both the sides.

Serve hot with the beaten curd. Add a little salt, roasted *jeera* and coriander leaves in the curd. This makes a hearty brunch for the family.

Ingredients
200 gms *methi*
150 gms *paneer* thickly grated
3 medium size boiled potatoes thickly grated
3 or 4 green chillies chopped
4 tsp coriander leaves chopped
6 tsp dry roasted *besan*
1 tsp salt
1 tsp coriander powder
1 tsp ground *anardana*
½ tsp aniseeds ground (*saunf*)
4 tsp finely chopped onions
½ cup crushed *bhujia*
3 or 4 tsp oil

METHI KEBAB

• *Servings 6 persons* • *Preparation time 25-30 mins.* • *Baking time 10-12 mins.*

- Separate leaves from *methi* and discard the stems. Finely chop them. Wash and squeeze the leaves dry.
- In a big bowl, mix together grated *paneer*, potatoes, onions, green chillies, coriander leaves, salt, coriander powder, *anardana*, *saunf* and roasted *besan*.
- Mix it and mash it till smooth like dough.
- With wet hands, take a small portion of the mixture. Make a round ball and flatten it lightly. Coat it with crushed *bhujia*. Similarly make all the *kebabs*.
- Grease a pan or a flat *tava* and lightly cook the *kebabs*.
- Roast them in pre-heated oven at 200°C for 10 minutes till nicely golden grown and crisp.
- Serve hot with mint chutney and onion rings.

Ingredients

6 medium sized par boiled potatoes

1 tsp salt, ¼ tsp turmeric powder

½ tsp red chilli powder

2 tsp dry coriander powder

½ tsp roasted and ground *jeera*, ½ tsp garlic paste

1½ ginger paste

3 tsp fresh lime juice

2 or 3 tsp oil

A pinch of sugar

Hung Curd Dip

½ cup hung curd

¼ tsp salt, 8-10 mint leaves chopped

1 or 2 green chillies chopped, ½ tsp sugar

1 tsp grated carrot

4 tsp cream

BATATA KEBAB

• Servings 6 persons • Preparation time + Marination tims 30 mins.
• Cooking time 10 mins. + Baking time 6-7 mins.

- Peel potatoes and cut them into 4 or 5 slices (½ inch thick each). Then rub all the ingredients on sliced potatoes. Refrigerate for half an hour.
- Grease a flat *tava* or a pan and rub one onion slice all over it to make it smooth and slippery.
- Heat the pan till smokey hot. Roast potatoes slices till golden brown. Sprinkle *chaat masala* and lemon juice.
- At the time of serving roast them in a pre-heated oven at 220°C for six to seven minutes.
- Serve immediately. Top it with hung curd dip, coriander leaves, red chilli powder and onion rings.

HUNG CURD DIP

- Mix all the ingredients. Put a blob of this dip on each roasted potatoes.

DAHI KE KEBAB

- *Servings 6 persons* • *Preparation time 15 mins.* • *Baking time 12 mins.*

Ingredients

1½ cups hung curd
200 gms *paneer* grated
2 green chillies chopped
4 tsp chopped coriander leaves, few mint leaves chopped
1 small onion finely chopped
½ cup finely chopped nuts and raisins
4 tsp bread crumbs, 1 level tsp salt
4 tsp *maida* and water as required

Contd.

HUNG CURD

- Hang one kg of curd in a wet muslin cloth for one hour. Lightly squeeze the cloth. The curd should be semi-solid.
- Mix together hung curd, *paneer*, green chillies, coriander leaves, onion, mint leaves, nuts and raisins, bread crumbs and salt till smooth.
- Shape the mixture into 20 small balls and flatten them.
- Mix water in 4 tsp of *maida* to make a thin batter like fresh cream.
- In a separate bowl mix all the ingredients of coating.
- Dip each ball in *maida* batter and coat with the prepared coating. Dust it and keep aside.

Contd.

Coating
1 cup dry bread crumbs
½ cup crushed cornflakes
½ tsp salt, ¼ tsp crushed garlic, 3 or 4 tsp finely chopped coriander leaves
1 tsp oil

- Pre-heat oven at 200°C for seven minutes and bake them at 220°C for 12 minutes till nicely golden brown.
- Serve with sauted onion, capsicum over lettuce bed.
- You can serve it with *roomali roti*.

Ingredients
4 medium size onions
½ tsp red chilli powder
½ tsp salt
4 tsp coriander leaves
4 tsp lemon juice
A pinch of sugar
A few strips of ginger

PYAAZ KE LACHCHE

• *Servings 5 persons* • *Preparation time 5 mins.*

- Cut onions into thin slices.
- Add salt, red chilli powder, coriander leaves, ginger strips, lemon juice and sugar.
- Thoroughly mix the ingredients and serve.

Tava Aalu, Arvi, Kamal Kakri ➢

 Overleaf Shashlik Vegetables on Saffron Rice

Ingredients
1 cup mint leaves
2 cup coriander leaves
1 onion, chopped
4 green chillies
4 or 5 garlic cloves
1" piece of ginger
1 raw mango
4 tsp *amchur* (mango powder)
1½ tsp salt
1 tsp sugar

PUDINA CHUTNEY

• *Servings 6 persons* • *Preparation time 10 mins.*

- Churn together mint leaves, coriander leaves, onion, green chillies, ginger, garlic and raw mango (if required) together till evenly ground. Add salt, sugar and *amchur* and again churn.
- Put in a serving bowl and serve.

LASUNIA CHUTNEY

Ingredients

2 or 3 peeled and grated garlic pods or ½ cup grated garlic
2 medium size grated onion
1 cup coriander leaves
1 tsp grated ginger
2 or 3 tsp oil
1 tsp red chilli powder
4 tsp sugar
½ tsp mustard seeds
½ tsp *kalonji* (onion seeds)
A pinch of *hing* (asafoetida)
A raw mango or 8 tsp vinegar

• *Servings 6 persons* • *Preparation time 15 mins.* • *Cooking time 5 mins.*

- Blend together onion, garlic, coriander leaves, ginger and raw mango or vinegar together.
- Heat oil in a pan. Add *hing*, mustard seeds and *kalonji* till the seeds crackle.
- Add red chilli powder and sugar; stir them.
- Add blended garlic and cook for four or five minutes.
- Cool and serve or fill in some bottle and use it.

BARBECUE DIP

• *Servings 6 persons* • *Preparation time 15 mins.*

Ingredients

2 tsp crushed garlic
2 tsp ginger paste
1 tsp salt
1 tsp red chilli powder
6 tsp oil
9 tsp vinegar
5 tsp castor sugar
3 or 4 finely chopped green chillies
6 tsp chopped coriander leaves
10 tsp tomato ketchup
¼ tsp cinnamon powder
½ tsp black rock salt

- Blend all the ingredients and pour in a serving bowl.
- Garnish with mint leaves and capsicum bits.

Ingredients
4 tsp black salt
4 tsp ground black pepper
4 tsp roasted and ground *jeera* (cumin seeds)
4 tsp *amchur* (mango powder)
¼ tsp cinnamon powder
1 tsp cardamom powder (crushed seeds)

TANDOORI MASALA

• *Servings 6 persons* • *Preparation time 10 mins.* • *Cooking time 5 mins.*

- Heat *tava* (griddle) and remove from fire. Put all the ingredients on the *tava* and stir.
- Grind all these for 15 seconds.
- Preserve this in an air-tight bottle.

Ingredients

20 button onions or 10 small onions chopped into two pieces
1 cup vinegar
2 tsp salt
½ tsp sugar
A pinch of sugar
Dry orange colour

ONIONS IN VINEGAR

• *Servings 6 persons* • *Preparation time 10 mins.* • *Cooking time 10 mins.*

- Cook vinegar, salt and sugar till lukewarm. Remove from fire. Cool.
- Touch your finger with dry orange colour and touch all the onion tops with it. Put them in a bottle and pour vinegar over these.
- Cover these tightly with the lid and shake.
- Use the onions after two hours.

GLOSSARY

Aata	—	Whole wheat flour
Ajwain	—	Caraway seeds
Amchur	—	Dry mango powder
Anardana	—	Dry pomegranate seeds
Arvi	—	Colocasia
Baigun	—	Brinjal
Belan	—	Rolling pin
Besan	—	Gram flour
Chaat masala	—	Spicy powder
Channa dal	—	Black gram lentil
Garam masala	—	Ground spices for seasoning
Ghee	—	Clarified butter
Gobhi	—	Cauliflower
Gulab jal	—	Rosewater

Hing — Asafoetida

Jeera — Cumin seeds

Kalonji — Onion seeds

Kamal kakri — Lotus stems

Kashmiri mirch — Red chilli from Kashmir

Kasuri methi — A special type of fenugreek seeds

Kathal — Jackfruit

Katori — Small, round container

Kebab — Cutlet

Kesar — Saffron

Khus khus — Poppy seeds

Lachcha — Layers or rings

Magaz — Melon seeds

Maida — Refined flour

Makhane — Dried lotus seeds

Malai — Top layer of cream on milk

Masala — Condiments

Mattar — Peas

Methi — Fenugreek seeds

Naan/Tandoori roti — Specal type of bread baked in a mud oven

Paneer — Cottage cheese

Pyaaz — Onion

Roomali roti — Extra thin bread specially prepared

Sarson — Mustard

Saunf — Aniseeds

Seekh — Skewer

Sigri — A small fire lighted in a basket

Suji — Semolina

Tava — Griddle

Tikkas — Cutlets